NeBU LOUS

VeRt IGO

RECENT AND SELECTED TITLES FROM TUPELO PRESS

The Radiant by Lise Goett
The Opening Ritual by G.C. Waldrep
The Right Hand by Christina Pugh
Called Back by Rosa Lane
Landsickness by Leigh Lucas
Green Island by Liz Countryman
The Beautiful Immunity
by Karen An-hwei lee
Small Altars by Justin Gardiner
Country Songs for Alice by Emma Binder
Asterism Ae by Hee Lee
then telling be the antidote
by Xiao Yue Shan
Therapon by Bruce Bond &
Dan Beachy-Quick
membery by Preeti Kaur Rajpal
How To Live by Kelle Groom
Sleep Tight Satellite by Carol Guess
THINE by Kate Partridge
The Future Will Call You Something Else
by Natasha Sajé
Night Logic by Matthew Gellman
The Unreal City by Mike Lala
Wind—Mountain—Oak: Poems of Sappho
by Dan Beachy-Quick
Tender Machines by J. Mae Barizo
Best of Tupelo Quarterly
Kristina Marie Darling, Ed.
We Are Changed to Deer at the Broken Place
by Kelly Weber
Why Misread a Cloud by Emily Carlson
The Strings Are Lightning and Hold You In
by Chee Brossy
Ore Choir: The Lava on Iceland
by Katy Didden and Kevin Tsang
The Air in the Air Behind It
by Brandon Rushton

NeBu LOus

VeRt IGo

Poems

BELLE LING

Tupelo Press
North Adams, Massachusetts

Nebulous Vertigo
Copyright © 2024 Belle Ling. All rights reserved.

ISBN-13: 978-1-961209-18-3 (paperback)
Library of Congress Cataloging-in-publication data available on request.

Cover and text design by Kenji Liu

Cover Art: Tsuchida Bakusen (1887—1936), "Ayu (Sweetfish)";
Yamatane Museum of Art, Tokyo, Japan.
Used by permission of Yamatane Museum of Art.

First edition May 2025.

All rights reserved. Other than brief excerpts for reviews and commentaries, no part of this book may be reproduced by any means without permission of the publisher. Please address requests for reprint permission or for course-adoption discounts to:

Tupelo Press
P.O. Box 1767
North Adams, Massachusetts 01247
(413) 664-9611 / Fax: (413) 664-9711
editor@tupelopress.org / www.tupelopress.org

Tupelo Press is an award-winning independent literary press that publishes fine fiction, non-fiction, and poetry in books that are a joy to hold as well as read. Tupelo Press is a registered 501(c)(3) non-profit organization, and we rely on public support to carry out our mission of publishing extraordinary work that may be outside the realm of the large commercial publishers. Financial donations are welcome and are tax deductible.

FOR MY PARENTS

CONTENTS

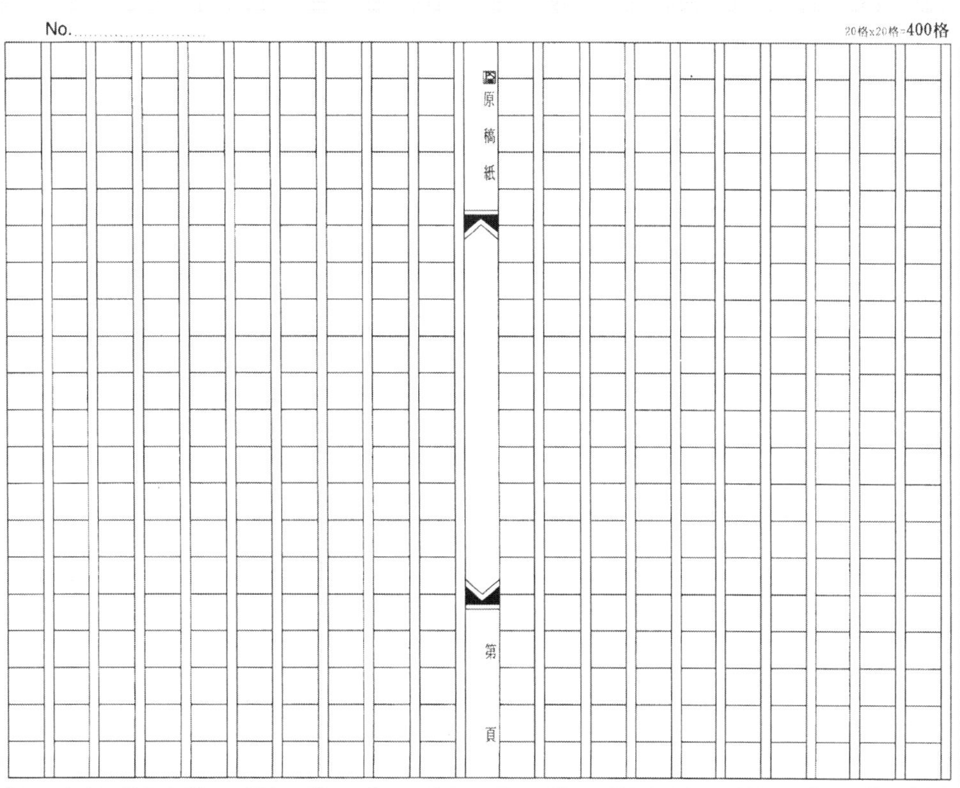
No.
20格x20格=400格
原稿紙
第
頁

It is always present within you.
You can use it any way you want.

—LAOZI

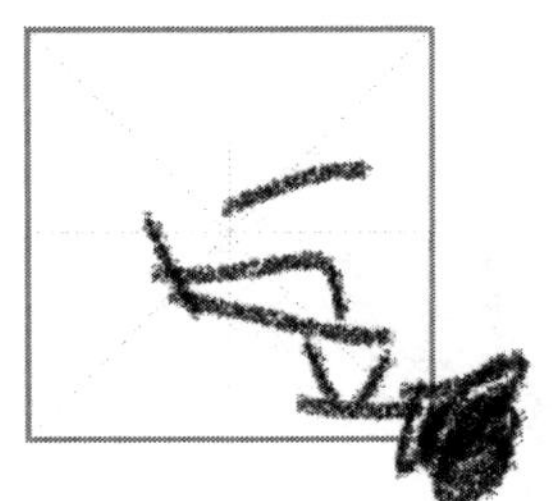

THIS LITTLE FISH

My face bears me like a mirror
          from its depth watching:

Here, I'm here—
          for years this yearning slaps,

yet it hardly breaks
          away from me by breaking

the full circle of what's
          been reflecting. See—

we're only strangers.
          You turn, for too, I'm

turning; you stay unbroken
          like a trap within me, and yet

not a rupture, ever,
          turns me away from being

tinier with you—for I'm
          caught unseen from within

turning. And again, through
          your tiniest titillations you

glow, like a big
        scheme of something—

bigger in my throat, saying:
        Come back, come back.

NEBULOUS VERTIGO

Too smooth—
I dare not climb over these drops:
circling, too cold, this milk.
After all, it's random in my gut,
                                        very quiet.

I sit close: it's muted
but turning; and a shard
floats to its very end, like a wrecked tip of goodwill—
too sharp,
                                                but hurray, hurray;

what's split
within me is a gastro-choke
        where the shock's burped, and the storm
girdling the drowned whose asymmetrical body
                                                        rowing, rowing—

Tomorrow, I'll look up
for more clarity; and now, glimpses—
                of my eyes in the nebulous vertigo between
                                                squawks, squawks.

BE QUIET IN THE MISO SOUP

This pond is a far province
    of many secrets: granules, granules,
        a forlorn fin slings a jut

of grit, of kelp, of stirs.
    Sparks poking the running
        of salt, of jaws, of soy.

I know not how a rill pleats
    a curd with so many curls
        that a slit on a tiny head grips

a rice grain that dissolves—
    but not quite—bridges the scent of rains
        and the ripples to come.

I know not from where these grains
    between a shape and a shattering shape,
        a riff-wave's surging

in sheaves, in blades, in wings—
    that clarity is a sharp spike—too much,
        or too little to know. Some say

pigs oaring around: Look at the lipids!
    Some say hens dropping eggs: Look,
        the yolk threads, languid yellow!

If there's too much, or too little
that makes me know not,
please let me go back—

to the centre of it all,
to sit, and to forget,
to sit, and to forget.

LET'S GO BACK TO GRASS FLOWER HEAD

豆:
one and a mouth and the shape of a horn.

Write this one-mouthed horn,
I was told. I was four, rains
taught me how to count things—
see, pantomime: 一 丨 ㄱ 一 丶 丿 一

Quiet! Teacher yells, *beans too near!*

Follow me! One vertical, one horizontal.
豆 squeaks its head out of the chalk.
Don't let 豆 *walk out of your square!*

Bean

DAU ^{2} / DAU ^{6}

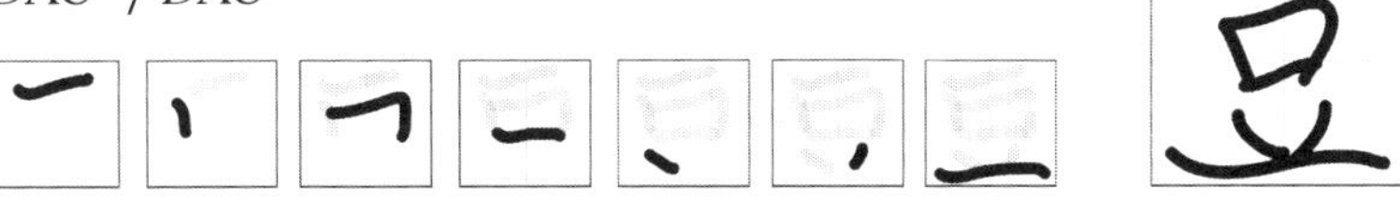

豆 grows 艹 in the rain.
Teacher calls it "Grass Flower Head."
It becomes 荳.
I've trouble with 艹,
Teacher tells me it's weed,
Mum says it's a ballerina's two little feet.

We are taught to sing: *Grass or flower?*
豆 *and* 荳 *and* 豆.
It is grass and it is a flower.
豆 *is* 荳 *is* 豆.
dau is tofu, tofu is *dau*.

I'm multiplied like window grids torn apart by the fingers of rains:

Every window looks out for 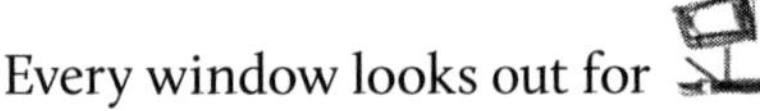

No! You write like chicken feet!
Your left slapping, your right smudges!

Imagine you’re 荳—

Let it tiptoe over your skin,
be porous in its breaths.

Breathe,
be ricocheted, be wings.

THIS HEART EATS

Rains studying pebbles,
                I reach out my hands—

Soft now, the night, fingertips
                to fingertips. How can I hide

if I'm already in the behind?
                July's seated, how parched—

I've never let a burden leave—
                Quick, pick up yourself!

Last year, our paper fans molten—
                now, the midnight askew,

You could've been better!
                One after another, this heart

eats to its content: I'm given back
                what I can't catch—

a circle after a square after a circle
                falling slack, my mind.

Grab tight! Eyes everywhere, tighter!
                Wanting more, these rains—

turn into a leaf, a fence,
                    a road of moonlights,

swallowing a star, a horse, a car—
                    sky after sky, to where?

63 TEMPLE STREET, MONG KOK

Remember 63 Temple Street, Mong Kok?
Remember that cha chaan teng,
Mrs. Suen, the owner?

Sorry, that jars your ears.
Remember "leave ice," "fly sugar leave milk," "tea go"—
the waiters' breaths, like shooting stars?

Sorry, again, for the monosyllabic dictums.
These imperatives chase me back
with their voracious tails to Mrs. Suen's cha chaan teng:

go, leave, fly.

Remember that deep-fried peanut toast—

a square button of butter, egg tassels,
slurry glass eyes of a honey stripe,
braided with sweet full-cream condensed milk?

Mrs. Suen uses Carnation's
condensed milk
from the contented cows of Australia
—as she says.

As for the peanut butter,
her preference is the USA's
Planters' Crunchy, their nuts clutter
but melt like mercy—as she says.

Remember me? Mrs. Suen asks.

Remember the already remembered?
All of us remember—
yet only some grasp the gyration of the remembered.

How can I not remember? Mrs. Suen!

For fifteen years the lukewarm TV gargles—
"Welcome to Hong Kong's Morning."
Every day I eat *deep-fried ghost*, drink *mandarin ducks*, no milk, no sugar.

A diet to keep myself forgotten.
I didn't forget you, Mrs. Suen remembers.

But all of us forget—yet only some let go of the forgotten.

How not to break the fluid egg yolk on my *doll noodles*?
Slightly tilt the egg's fringe

up with your chopsticks and pinch—
but the translucent membrane still cracks.

It doesn't forget the way to brokenness, and neither do I.

Grandma sipped the braised pork belly,
her last ritual in the hospital.

The rain breaks its back,
reaches out its little hands,
and cut them off in front of me.

Follow me, it says.
And just as I follow, it vanishes, and multiplies.

Here's my mobile number, I
forgot yours! Mrs. Suen recalls.

Laozi says: "She forgets it.
That's why it lasts forever."
Did she trade her memory for
the eternity of my number?

The rain finds its path to
remember, and falls upon every
person,

wanting—

I: *One tea set, please.*
WAITER KUEN: *Tea set's sold out.*
I: *A fast set, then.*
WAITER KUEN: *No fast set today.*
I: *I'd have a constant set, anyways.*
WAITER KUEN: *Constant set is fast set, fast set is tea set.*

a fate of return—the rain and Waiter Kuen's back.

Now the rain's a searchlight: a black dog sniffs, a black car follows.
There's no way to see how rain enters.

You still have much black hair, Mrs. Suen, I grin.

Rain stumbles upon its hands, grips a larger surround.

Thanks to the braised pork belly, Mrs. Suen laughs.

> *O, O, what a slice!* Grandma exclaimed.
> The fat broke loose on her tongue.
> She never woke up again.

A raindrop, very quiet on my lips.
It melts into a shore afar—to where?

A red bean sneaks out of my glass.
I lick it back—to where?

I forget to give Mrs. Suen my mobile number.
The rain has no proper path to rise back as rain.

How does hunger enter me?

I forgot the first bite in my life.
I forget why I forgot.

Coolness sprawls flat on my tongue.
I can't even give it a name.

DINING WITH WHOM?

The sky watches like yesterday.
The stars haven't finished predestining.

Dinner comes, windows can't eat.
The door refrains from closing.

Candles burning their bruised eyes:
"I, the anonymous I."

The floor dares not step forward—
that's why I move closer to the table.

Around the corner the air beckons:
"Can you come back tomorrow?"

But for whose tomorrow I'm waiting?
And, I ponder, tomorrow who'll stay

so fastidiously like you here with me—
that you, regardless, in the spacious,

keep surrounding this I, the solitary I?
Stay well, my dear. You can't flee

I, the intriguing I—and even now
just as I breathe, I nearly hit you—

CONTEMPLATING THE COD

Remember that short dusk:
a cod skirted around the groove—
it was certainly a slippery hope

to the rock—I'd seen it dancing.
But I couldn't spy
its spine when the sun spun.

And now in the freezer,
It's a cold ghost that doesn't shrink.
It has no clue why it builds frost—

Fish speak fear in an emotional fever;
they'd move to warmer water
to have their temperature raised because they burn
up in stress. Like me,
they can suffer—

Before I lay my hands to rinse
the cod and skewer its gill,
I want to feel, again, with my bare fingers—
the estranging, flimsy, long-sighed drip of damp—

You've travelled a long way.
I am sorry.

SORRY, SORRY

Again, upon the edge
          of a blue square inch—
that the water's fixing, I see

the waves convulse,
          like aching in a *no-no*.
Within the cracks of the rocks

where the water can't escape,
          a gap in the mud nudges—
sorry, I hear; then your hand

pushes me like an existential
          sorry extending you—
towards the laborious middle

of buoyancy: the water
          and its various blue
veins where the dark

reappears; and there, the carps
          sailing against the assailing—
my shadow, cut shallow

between your lips: *Sorry*. We're
          stricken with slits, shining.
A few ducks shriek so loud

that I'm afraid their brains
almost overpour. And now,
everywhere, merely pores;

and I, with no clue, why I'm
being gouged among these
bright sorrows under the sun.

Yet, already underneath,
however deep—
there, a bait's hung, and it's

tilting up; its tiny arc
tightly pulled, plumbing
you—

WHAT ARE YOU, REALLY?

Think *bowl* as a circumference—
turn your finger clockwise.

Or, try another way:
step back to evade anything

that's disappearing—
this *bowl*, very serene.

Wheel your neck to feel
you, yourself.

Strain your face—
Keep on, circle this *bowl*:

See the subterranean fires?
The glaring gyres engulfing

your copper-red body
with much haemorrhaging—

Keep your eyes closed:
Come closer, to anything.

Refrain from what you've
been thinking of. Fill

the *bowl* to the brim. Spill
it. Reappear—

like nothing's happened—
Now, this *bowl* is you.

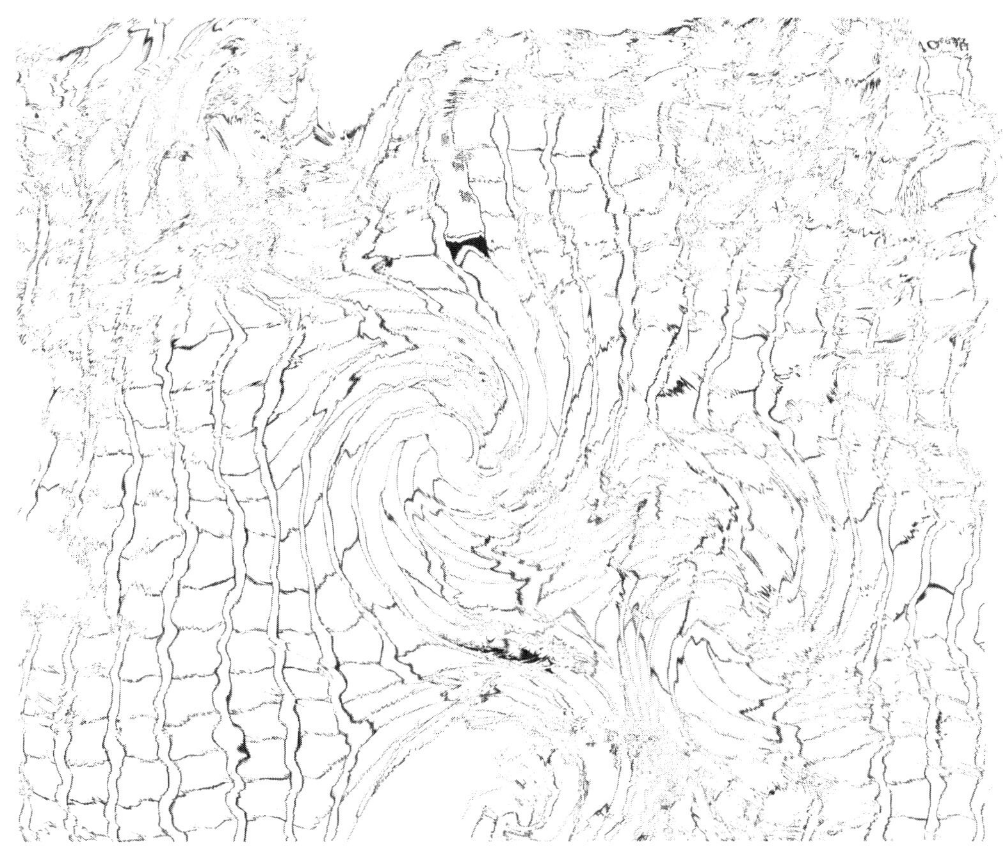

THIS YEAR THE SKY

in Paris is interpreted—
with horror, horse, and stethoscope.
In April, people say:
love conquers all. In May,
when Venus is in sextile to Neptune,
my lover wishes for a break-
through; or a semi-break,
if a meteorite interrupts
the Saturn's orbit.

Content to be charmed,
our horse bathes in its cabochon jade;
the green, an illusion of grass—
my bracelet, self-deception.
It was, as you told me, inspired
by Zhinü and Niulang,
who, separated for three hundred
and sixty-four days,
reunite over the star Deneb
on the seventh day
of the seventh lunar month.
This will happen in August—
once in every year.

Once, you told me
you're governed by the moon—
turquoise, your energy stone.
You carry it like your pulse,

let it tell you—
to love or not to.
In December,
one out of billion
photons disturbs your mood;
and you let the turquoise
centre your mind
around that space, the origin
of stars, planets, rocks.

A HINTERLAND WITHIN UNCLE'S FENG SHUI MIRROR

January curls its limbs, I hear it pulling a nerve.

I've travelled weeks to this headache.

Hardest to mirror: the missed and the missing.

Typhoon days: boundaries circling with no intervals.

A few preserved plums upon my tongue.
Ice-cubes cluttered with classical clarity in the glass.

"Flower" spelt "rewolF" in Uncle's mirror—
In the mirror there appears an invisible shore with a new border.

This octagonal Feng Shui mirror, says Uncle, *is for dispelling evils.*

How so, Uncle?

To the north, the birds set off.

This is how fate mirrors: no territory's owned but margins mirrored from trillion angles.

Days after days, fate chirps like an untamed bird.
Birds poop on Uncle's Feng Shui mirror.
A twangy-silent prosperity?

For years I talk to a stranger in our telephone who intrigues me like a mirror:

> *Is your Uncle here?* / I: *Who're you?*
> *I've a dragon fruit for him.* / I: *You know him?*
> *My fruit sold out quick.* / I: *Sorry, he doesn't like fruit.*

Banana leaves magnet spirits, murmurs Uncle, cleaning his Feng Shui mirror.

Behind a towering line of banana trees lurks a red brick house.

Uncle's mirror can't tamper our house's Feng Shui after being trimmed by the sun.

> *Your Uncle likes me, so he'd like my dragon fruit.* / I: *I'm not sure if he likes you.*

The same stranger's befriended our telephone years after years.
Not easy to end your fate, Uncle says.

For how long will I be seen? The sun's been accruing glints—
this afternoon has no end.
And the seen returns unkempt in the mirrored lights.

On my desk: two cartons of Vita Lemon Tea.

Empty stomach empty noise empty corridor: nothing's here for the mirror to pinpoint.

Drink some sencha, mosquitoes tipsy.
    I won $6000 with King Fairy Prawn, boasts Uncle.
                                        But that Dusty Light killed me.

Yesterday, King Fairy Prawn came last.

                        Next time, I'll pick a muscular horse.

Every day, the clock ticks out the ephemeral for being
                                        eternally locked to the numerals.

How the sun trespasses the seen: drowsiness.

This January, a familiar voice wants an unusual attention from our phone—
I know what you want. / I: *Sorry, I don't know you.*

From my plate sputters a carnivorous dichotomy—
Uncle: *Prawns or pork? Want more of what?*

Prawns buried under pork hardly elude their predestination flavoured with sauce—

Raw not good, Uncle pushes me his prawns simmered in oyster-ketchup.

Mustard-yellow roes in his rotten prawns' heads.
I wonder if they're too burdened.

You know we too shall pass, whispers Uncle.

Uncle: *Pork shreds or Prawn thatches?* / I: *Prawns' legs here, too gluey, unpickable.*

Ripped, drowning paths, these typhoon days.

Not a thing's brutal here, Uncle wipes his Feng Shui mirror.
To tame fear is to mirror it, to mirror is to stay here—

I'm sure you took the green apple, groans Uncle, rubbing the green stains off his mirror.

I: *Four green apples in a red bowl?* / I: *Four red apples in a green bowl?*

TV: 大門外有蟋蟀　迴響卻如同幻覺

No, Uncle, it was a red apple.

Pellucid corners in the mist, crickets flee as I'm trying to explain.

TV: 就算牙關開始打震　別說謊

You don't need to lie, reiterates Uncle.

My apple, unapologetically
stolen, my mouth falls unto *so – so*.

Bulbous as usual:
I look around—every day the sun moves

around the same spot, and there,
a bird comes:
it pecks at the same apple,
dumps it, and picks
it up again.

Our broken phone remembers nothing it's heard last night:

What do you want? / I: *What do I want?*
I: *And so?* / *And so what?*

Too quick: no apology but only squeaks from the dark,
are they from the phone or the bird?

The tree, the bird, the wind,
tongue-rhymed.

Bird, let me have my portion—
or be mine.

Not a bird's seen on the Feng Shui mirror after typhoon.

How can I make whole the lights shattered by the mirror?

Humble joy:
not knowing how
the sun shines us into strangers and and licks my ears—

Look!
Hey bird, can you be my balloon?

EVERY MORNING

Every morning you hug me
like you've nobody to love.
But I believe in your hug—

like every morning's juggling
the trajectories of you. You
ask me to pray before eating

every morning. You say that God
says: *faith isn't sight*; so I pray
by smelling your body as you

move over me like butter—
for every morning you can't love
without brushing my leg, asking:

my love, where's love?
You smell by kissing, you
muster a matrix upon my body—

What a coward, you whisper,
how many days God's given
me you that you're still afraid

of having somebody to love—
Every morning, I promise to give you
more; for every morning I'm not scared

of handling you in the unresolved,
        as you check my shadow. But you're
                leaving; please, I'll give more, more—

TENDER DISTURBANCE

Up, up—Mum caves in—
There, there
Look! I'm circling
water with semi-
circles. *Mum, Can I grip*
water? Mum gives me a glass
of water, she doesn't
understand.
See
how much we're given, says Mum.
Stunt-seconds—
our roof doesn't understand.
Water teaches us supermarket's
plastic bags in opalescent
water- moods—
See, water's growing more fingers.
Who needs more water?
Our dogs just fed. Flies,
everywhere; million reds
from our watermelon slices falling
for a fruitier-sweeter apparel—
Ennui, ennui, can I hold you?
Water's counting ennui.
Down, down!
Meaningless, meaningless!
Our fan, one metre
above us, excited.
The rain pauses,

cicadas cascade. I fling
my eyes to hook
a slice of moon back
to an equipoise, and listen—
the fan pendulums.

TASTING KARMA

Does the doctor prefer eating an apple
before announcing death? Mrs. Suen's mother
died of liver cancer. The doctor says:
"Just so—sorry." Sow, her mother preferred
sow, the honey-motherly winey odour.
One sunny day, Mrs. Suen's mother couldn't stop
eating apples. For fifteen years, the doctor
advised: "I don't know." One day, Mrs. Suen's
mother stopped eating: "So, so—" Soul,
a metaphysical volta, inedible. Are days
after death "days"? The doctor repeats: "More apples!"
Mrs. Suen feels her mother in her barbecued sow,
and she vomits all night like Typhoon Koto.
Her mother liked her pork belly drenched
in a pool of leeks, onions, and garlic.
"Grease breeds bliss, greed feeds greed—
good reaps good, bad reaps bad," said her mother.
Mrs. Suen's mother distained apples
for they exaggerated quasi-idealism.
Three hundred years ago, the debt wasn't paid,
"Tell me, will I be your daughter in my next life?"

LET YOUR HAIR BE GONE

"More black hair, more luck!"
Mr. Yuen's very proud of his hair—
"Good energy, ah, ah, my hair!"

TV: Let your yesterday's hair
be yesterday's hair

"My hair storms
rains clawing," Mr. Yuen hardly brings
forth any meanings, he's too anxious: "Typhoon lost my umbrella!"

"Typhoon! Kuen!—" Mr. Yuen's turning impatient.
"Kuen, are you listening?"

TV's listening but Kuen isn't.
The TV mirrors Mr. Yuen but the TV isn't
a mirror and the mirror isn't Mr. Yuen.

"I stare into the mirror every day.
Mirror doubles energy!" Mr. Yuen turns to Mrs. Suen.

"Is there a mirror-longevity golden ratio," Mrs. Suen
turns back, puzzled, "like one inch closer,
one year younger?"

Waiter Kuen: "Me and this mirror, too broken, no use!"
The TV mirrors me and me mirrors the TV.

Struggling against the invisible—
is how Mr. Yuen being mirrored in the TV
forces the TV mirroring more of Mr. Yuen.

Kuen: "Listen—my daughter's been stuck
on a hospital bed for thirteen years; she's too quiet, like Hello Kitty!"

"Focus, Kuen!" yells Mrs. Suen.
Mr. Yuen tidies his hair, focuses on the natural order:

first, macaroni with ham,
then a monkey-picked oolong tea,
and after that, there arrives *sai doi si*—

Mr. Yuen's favourite is *sai doi si.*

"Two corned beef sandwiches! Yellow's the morning!"
Mrs. Suen's solace is always colourful.
Her mother passed away yesterday.

Her family name "Suen" 孫 passes
"suen-ness" over to her offspring. So,
Mrs. Suen mirrors Mrs. Suen's mother; so
Mrs. Suen likes studying
her mother's mirror. Sow, her mother likes sow.

Mr. Yuen: "Typhoon, oh, my fish!"
"Who needs more hair?"

Sai doi si touches Mr. Yuen's hair:
cirrus whites, fragile delights.

"More black hair, more luck!"
Mr. Yuen's *sai doi si* can't be luckier after touching his fake black hair.
TV: Let your hair be gone,
there's no right or wrong—

Kuen: "My daughter, Koto, loves frogs;
she's a fan of Kerokerokeroppi, not Hello Kitty."

Hello Kitty can't appeal, it has no mouth.
How long has Hello Kitty not uttered "hello"?

Kuen: "Hello Kitty—a girl like a cat? A girl or a cat?
A girl-cat or a cat-girl?"

"My little Koto wondered why no typhoon's called Kerokerokeroppi."
Mr. Yuen: "Because Kerokerokeroppi—
isn't as obedient as our little Koto."
"Because—" says Mrs. Suen, "there's no because—
just a day lost to another day."

Mrs. Suen chucks the paper cups away,
pats Mr. Yuen's shoulder.
TV and the mirrored TV,
the TV mirrored in the opposite mirror.

Kuen: "What date is today?"

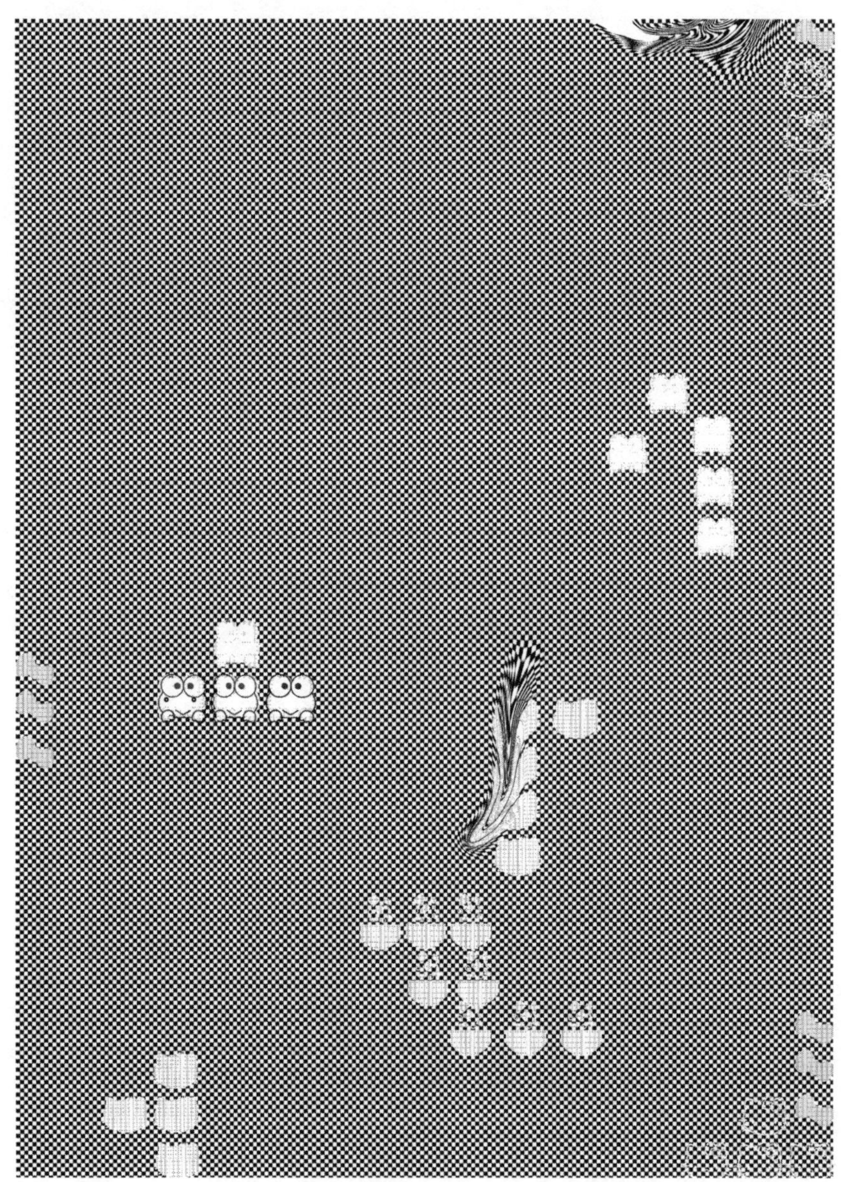

SPEED ODE

O allegro, O accelerando, O vivacissimo,
please, thalamus and hypothalamus,
stop exaggerating my unappeased tempo!
My lover says if I can't be with him now
he'll probably give himself to another—
O no, not for sex, but for maturity; no, not for maturity,
but for true love indeed; and he'll, probably,
never forget me too *quickly*. O allegro con spirito,
O molto allegro, O allegretto maestoso!
What a torrent when he greets my ears
Suzuki and my nose Asashi! The identical beat
hurries me to love *this, this, this*
of his, while I'm still doubting *that, that, that* of his
promises like *I will wait, I will try, I will give*.
See, how love whips his jelly-squishy lips.
Feel me, he kneels. I'm not familiar with him,
so I'm not familiar with how to feel him—
Adagio ma non troppo, moderately slow but not
too slow, yet his *moderato* is already *allegretto*.
Please, let me finish my study, I beg.
Keep me please, like dating clouds, he pleads.
His body, like a curve in the smoke, rises
into a red-green skyline that I can hardly
enter—even with my *largo*. O largo!
Open me tenderly, he croons, *petite and dolce*,
like splitting a chrysalis. I get up
and howl: *Wait!* He: *For what?*
Quick, butt, say I fuckin' love you;

otherwise, he'll say: *My ex-fiancée wants a family.*
O Scarlatti, O Shostakovich, tell me, tell me,
how fast is *allegro*, how relentlessly should I give
so love would relax its feet for me to paddle along?

MISS WONG SAYS

I.

Say */dau /*,
row your lips sideways,
then oar an orb—
now 豆 is you.
豆: a red bean for you to hold.
Hold it tight,
you'll be whole.

Say */dau /*,
豆's yearning for */dau/*
Look: a round red bean!
Seong Si, "Shared Yearning"
Red beans skitter in the south,
How many of them will be kept?
Take more, my dear friend,
Let them whisper between us.

/dau/daui/dou/,
your tongue—a pool
of nihilistic sweat.
Break */dau/daui/dou/*,
your mouth—
豆's dopamine, 豆's doppelgängers.

2.

It's not like this! Miss Wong says.
But her 豆, how maudlin!
The spirit of her 豆 has probably
darted off.
Miss Wong's Grandpa suffering
in her 豆's posture,
coughs: *O, no, no!*

3.

豆 / *dau* /:

Do you prefer an implausible emptiness burning
or a tofu brooding with its frozen pores?
Here—we only have the imprint of a bright page.
One hazy afternoon my nose's bleeding.
I've always loved a malty soy drink: 豆奶.
豆 is Vitasoy, bottled.

4.

For hundreds of years, in her past lives
Miss Wong's Grandma's survived
hunger as a dog, a boar, a frog.

After years, in a high-rise apartment,
she's now chewing 豆
stewed in her *ma po dau fu* casserole,

moaning: *too salty.*

5.

Eraser's residuals, braided,
my 豆
Duplicates, too many delusions,
my 豆
For how many times I've curved myself
inward onto
this 豆?
豆, you, at the corner or in the centre? 豆,
Where're you?

6.

Write 豆, says Miss Wong,
This is your fate: iteration.

豆 cries every day.
Miss Wong's Grandma eats
too much 豆; and she cries:
No, no.

7.

A self with a multitude of selves:
I'm the one-hundred-written 豆—
a silenced mantra.

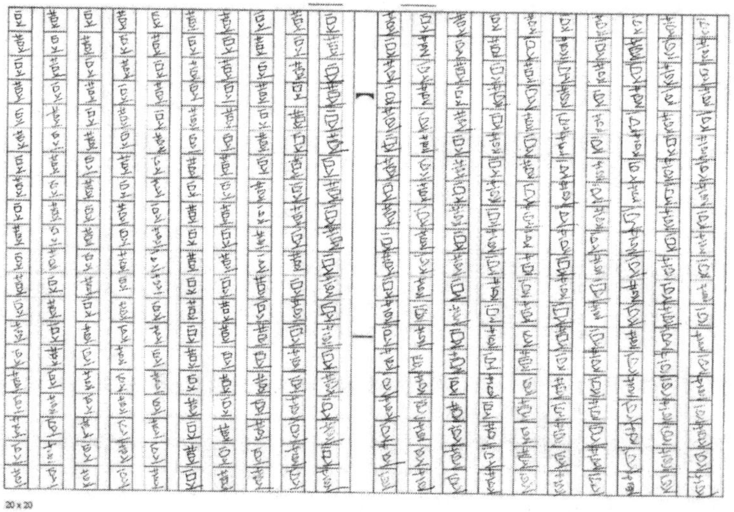

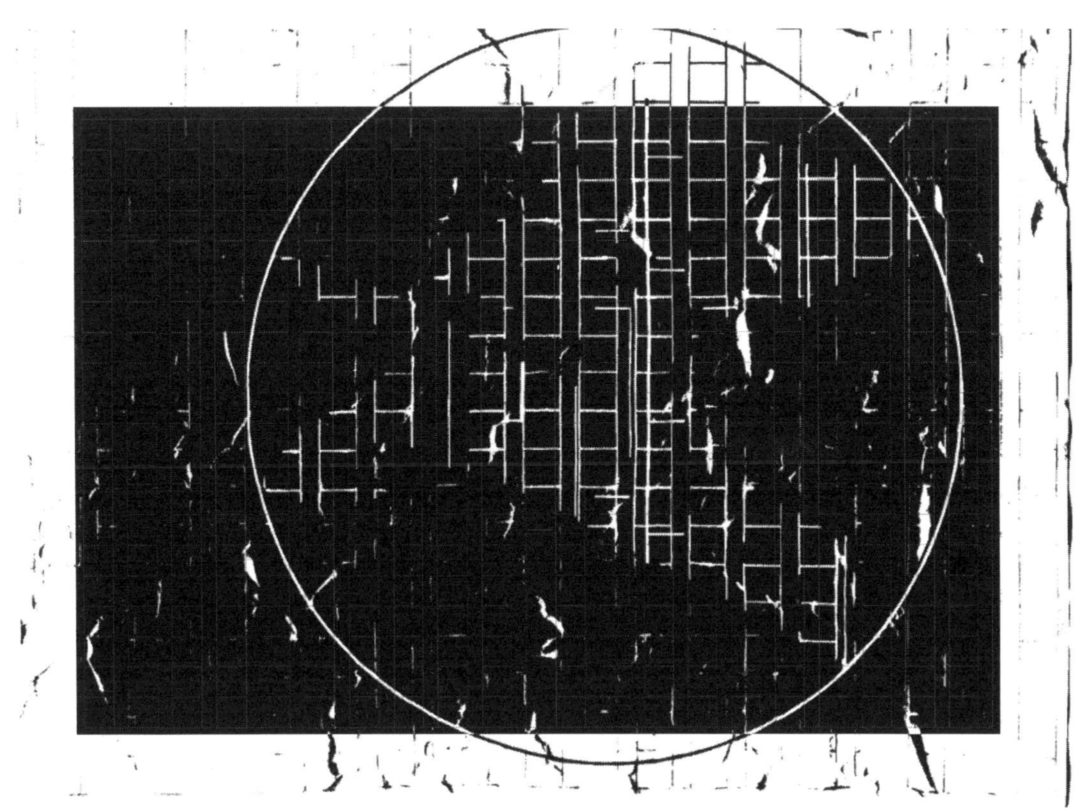

SO, IS THAT HOW LIGHT TRAVELS?

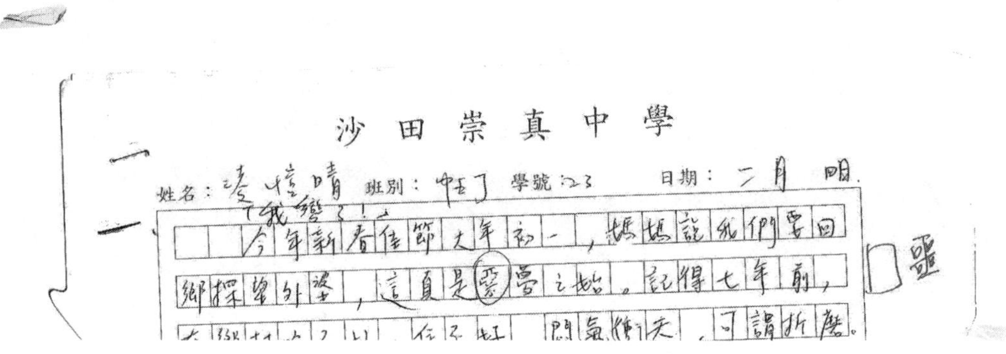

沙田崇真中學

姓名： 班別： 學號： 日期：

今年新春佳節大年初一，媽媽說我們要回

鄉探望外婆，這真是惡夢之始。記得七年前，

噩

One night, I got married multiple times.
Anyhow, it wasn't a nightmare.
Well, not a nightmare in its traditional sense.

惡夢, I write.
噩夢, Miss Wong writes.

惡夢 or 噩夢? These are the capsules that a "nightmare" can't crack.

The former revisits a dream with disgusting contents.
The latter— according to Miss Wong—
revitalizes the aura of a nightmare
which unmercifully declares my 惡夢 is wrong.

I wrote in an essay later: *This Lunar New Year,*
we're heading back where Grandma lives.
This is the beginning of my 惡夢—

"I've told you, it's 噩夢," stresses Miss Wong.
"But even the moon can't tell if my dream is 噩夢 or 惡夢," rebuke I.

Often with a square she marks,
as if she can't live without
penning herself a square which's the draft
of a new window in her new house.

Her new window beckons rewriting 惡夢 into 噩夢.

The long train ride towards Grandma's village
roars through a wild boar forest—
On the windowpane my eyes get lost.

That's how dreams vacate the path towards right or wrong.

As usual, several nightmares are looking
towards the window; and while they turn back,
they're beaming, like knowing me years ago.

The seat, originally assigned to me, is somehow—
occupied by a traveller who's crying.

In this case, the moon emits an eerie shine.

"When dreams are shocked, that's '噩,' the origin
of dissonance, as written in *The Rites of Zhou*," told Miss Wong,
"'噩' is horror; and hence, 'nightmare' is '噩夢.'"

But horror is when behind a person her shadow
bearing uncertainties for the next move—

And, when I walk closer, her shadow
flows; or, just as I let it flow and up it goes—

The moon then reappears as if it's in a correct dream.

Is it 噩夢 or 惡夢?

"Too many mouths," I tell Miss Wong.

"They're looking out for nothing but someone useless like you—"
Miss Wong shrieks, yet she's not dying.
I can't find my mouth in all my writing.

I stuff more rabbitless white rabbit candies into my mouth.
There's a depth within me snared in vain.

"噩夢, you need to suck it in so you'll fly," reasserts Miss Wong.

噩夢 and 惡夢 in my mouth, hollowing me into echoes.

I start writing again: *This year, days are withering,*
I've gone far into the deep south for Grandma.

I've wandered to a where that can't bear my pain.

Then, I hear Zhuangzi saying: "Now, in the mist
you're a large tree, why not be planted
in the middle of nowhere? For something—
that's useless will never be destroyed."

I remember how Miss Wong shrieks herself into a huge bare tree.
No mistakes will ever bother her, nor shorten her days.

I'm eager to see if my dream's 惡夢 or 噩夢.

I look towards the sky and the moon whispers: *I'll come back tomorrow.*
Yet, the reality is: it's arrived yesterday.

Bitterness rests in my stomach so it's not going to revolt.

"If you're willing to be dreamt, you'll be dreamt," says Grandma.
"What if I'm unwillingly dreamt?" I wonder.

Grandma looks down to her hands, she murmurs,
"That's why I've ridded my rod of hooks!"

惡夢 is never a correct dream.

The moon looks into my eyes.
The rabbit within me has a light to shine.

JESUS GREEN, CAMBRIDGE

The earth now shrinks into an arrow.
This is the way, walk in it—

It's winter. The park's coughing frost.
The trees crawl into mercury.

The gate of Jesus College every year
guides us: *Walk right, turn west—*

We turn into faithful followers,
albeit the gate's painted darker.

Slightly left, and finally continue
onto St. John's Road. And yet—

after Jesus no prophecy's allowed—
St. John by all means forbids wi-fi.

We move back to our every step—
Isaac Newton's First Law of Motion:

Stay moving unless pushed or pulled.
The earth moves every satellite to fall

towards itself without making it hit
the ground. Always, there's a force.

Jesus Green, the perennial green
on our screen centring us, says:

Be not dismayed—

TO BEGIN AGAIN

"One early morning the lake
smooth like a porcelain,
I see a lady eating her toast.
Arrows after blue arrows,
she never swims back, her toast
clean as a tabula rasa."

This is one of his stories.
By telling me stories he feels alive.

Sometimes, for a plot twist,
the shrimp gets strangled,
its torso's juiced with pink;
the ocean, calm and blue.

"The next morning," he says,
"a bruise on her neck, no pain.
She flexes, and feels like ether,
her arms, her legs, reaching far—"

We lay like two coffins on bed:
"Fear not, for Thou are with me.
Fear not, for I'll strengthen you."

He likes reciting Bible's verses
and tells me death stories.

“On the opposite shore,” he says,
everything’s veiled, the shore—
only a faint blue head;
yet, from afar, I’d hear her
when I’m throttled.”

Deep in the dark I stare
into his chest long enough
to have my shadow sunk.
Along with my eyes, I’ve been—
rummaging my innermost
opulent shadow to float.

A TANGERINE

Pit scrapes pit—
viscous, my head;
Face—a soft pad of pinholes.

What a loser I am, yes!—
How sour I'm—
like guilt.

Got stolen, my nerves—
how can I even grieve?

Blown up, for whom?
Ah, where's my neck?
I kneel, I can't sleep—

Stand up! White thin shreds!
Stay here!
Let the observed multiply—
And you stay here!

TOFU FLOWER WITH RED BEANS

The void inside eats the void
        outside—tofu never feels full.

                Uncle Ming's staccato cubicle:
Red beans! Foo yu, yu foo,
        yau dau foo. Need? No need?

A palm-sized watery cube
                very quiet in the red bucket—   *Yours lum,*
one lum tofu please, and five dollars
        of five-spice pan-dried tofu slices,

        yours gau lum. I'd nag Mum
to add a bowl of tofu flower.
        Sauce, yes? No? My whole

        afternoon stranded in the toilet. Too much
                hoisin sauce, Sriracha,
and Uncle's Tai O black bean paste.

Attendance crossed out. Miss Wong:
                Write 豆
        one hundred times, hand it over by 7a.m.

TEMPLE BELL

Three sets you free.
Four is death.

Five stumbles.
One is embarrassing—

Only one strike,
how lonely, like a widow.

How about two?
Two mirrors—

Strike it hard,
let the wind strike back.

THIS JULY TOTORO

This July, brother plucks a cornstalk
the same size as his thigh. It's a summer
after sunshower, the dying
sleep in half-lights, their faces—

turning into mysteries under the sun.
Our faces, says Borges, pass like water—
for we're always leaving the shivers
of our own phantoms around circling.

My face, already, plundered by the sun—
for the bright has passed me on
from one shore to another; and yet, still—
I'm being envisaged within the bright

shimmers. And soon, by the ocean, I see
the art of mirroring and relinquishing
me: I'm hollowed out like currents—
just after somebody's breathed his last.

"Hello, moshi-moshi? I pick up the phone.
What's arrived soon dies in echoes.
Someone's been waiting, and so am I.
"Your Uncle's probably arrived—" says Mum.

"Gomen nasai, say it again?" I'm puzzled.
"Your Uncle's probably drinking mist—"
What Mum probably means is that Uncle's
probably arrived because he's released

from this world to survive in another realm.
In the midst, I'm undivided, waiting—
"Hai, moshi-moshi? Do you hear me?"
Often, our phone picks up a few puzzles

for voices to turn and return like echoes—
yet, times and again, they're changing;
and so, just as I've reckoned, at least
for a moment, they're from somewhere

which's too far away that even the present
simply touches me in vain on this earth.
"July 21st, your Uncle's birthday!"
Our phone's waiting, and too I'm waiting.

"Hai! You listening? Moshi-moshi?"
Only are humans welcomed in the phone.
"Chotto matte - chotto matte . . ."
The phone hears me, yet I hear nothing.

To the phone, I must be too imperfect,
and quietly the phone recedes to an object.
"Out! Out! You, Makkuro Kurosuke!"
Brother, again, talking loud to the TV.

"Does Makkuro Kurosuke live upstairs?
asks brother. "Ghost even lives in my beer!"
Here, again, Uncle talks like a crisp-thrill
ghost from his bubbling Asahi Super Dry.

"If you die, you'll certainly live forever . . ."
How many times Uncle sounds he's died!
"So, remember," stresses Uncle, "always
say 'moshi-moshi'; for only is one 'moshi'

released by the dead's shuttered throat.
If you're greeted by one 'moshi' and you
turn around, you'll have your soul stolen!
So—double your 'moshi'! Don't ever let

yourself get near Sanzu!" So, afterwards,
with what I've reckoned, as humans
we're to repeat: "I'm going to do the dishes
tomorrow after tomorrow after tomorrow."

"Tomorrow, your Uncle's birthday!"
Often, our phone breathes so far as I do—
and so far as mum speaks, I've to nod.
And once, I was told that the deceased

would pay their debt by crossing the rapids
of Sanzu—so our demeanours while alive
on this earth would determine whether we'd
tread across a bridge or a ford or the snake-

afflicted waters with terror to our afterlife.
Our TV's yelling, and too brother's yelling:
"Where's Makkuro Kurosuke going to?"
"To the kids like you who're not obeying—"

If you're brave enough to lean over the dead,
you'd see that near to their eyebrows glows—
an eternal glint which even the dead body
can hardly steal away with its mortality.

"Keep quiet and say sorry," commands Uncle.
"So, I'll be given a heaven's ticket?" I retort.
Every other day, a stranger calls, asking how
he can deliver his self-grown dragon fruit.

"Moshi-moshi, your Uncle birthday's coming!
How should I give him my dragon fruit?"
"Chotto matte - chotto matte . . ."
The stranger's gone, just as I'm to reply . . .

The sky's revolving, and too I'm revolving.
Days after days, I'm wakened—
by urgent calls, nameless calls, random calls.
Too many phone calls, after Typhoon Rondo.

"Your very first lesson, remember," reminds
Uncle, "is that after you die, you need to see
if you can still mutter 'moshi – moshi'!
See if you'd be mercifully revived . . ."

In goodbyes the phone hides no tremors,
there've been traumas behind murmurs—
whereas from my throat flees a rupture:
"Will I see you again after this life?" I wonder.

"Shush, shush," Makkuro Kurosuke hurries.
Makkuro Kurosuke's eyes too big in the TV.
Yet, nothing appears too small in whispers.
By ringing me the phone ripples out like rain—

I hear nothing but only the rain crying:
"I'm full and empty, empty and full . . ."
The sky has no smallest delight in sorting out
why on this earthly side it's always raining—
On the other side, somebody keeps calling:
"Wait! Wait!" I'm in the river, crossing
over to the other side. Turning back, I'm almost
swallowed by the river, and I keep yelling—

"Moshi-moshi, moshi-moshi!" Rain, rain,
what're you devouring for your appetite?
I keep my mouth open for more rain—
for only the living attracts that much rain.

"Excuse me, may I have a shadow-free coffee?"
That evening, Borges comes over for a coffee.
To Borges, however, it's certainly morning.
"Sorry, sir," I apologize, "it's really late—

to prepare whatever coffee that you may like—"
To be honest, I'd like to ask him about
his poem wherein that a prisoner keeps writing
about how Borges keeps writing about him—

in return makes Borges keep writing for years.
Borges, amused by his shadow, leaning forth
in the dark of my shadow, murmurs:
"Please let me finish drinking this instant!"

Meanwhile, he whispers: "it's really a grace
being half-erased." Since then, I'm amazed—
by how little I'm allowed to remember his visit:
I'm forbidden to rekindle any dimming blaze.

Within the dark, the rain never falls asleep:
"Chotto matte - chotto matte . . ."
How I revere every little rain steadily
moves the dark from one stare to another.

The next day, the sun comes, somebody sighs:
"Ah, this heart eats, this heart eats!
Gooey puru puru. Sugoi na!"—
"Idiot, your Uncle's last words," shouts Mum,

"Quick, burn your Uncle more red chillies."
"Gaebul, O, gaebul, oishi, oishi! Chomped!
Fat pink hoku-hoku—" exclaims Uncle.
Tell me, how many red chillies should I burn?

Arise! You red hot chillies relentlessly sipping
the gochujian's vertigo: "Oishi, oishi!"
Two, are you sorting out your opponent?
One, are you being your own companion?

Every summer, in mid-July, as I remember,
we'd visit a green wing called the Totoro Forest—
near Tokorozawa in Saitama, where lilies,
the vanilla ones, relaxingly, chill in breeze.

The trees around, leafy and green, in a cool
play with the red-tattered flowers and bees.
Colours strolling, like carefree vagabonds—
the breeze along with us, a generous giver.

Not far, I see a leafy chestnut tree, Uncle
says: "This tochi-no-ki cures cattle's coughs
and horses' heaves, and surely, different kinds
of bruises and sprains, and too, diarrhoea—

and no doubt, nostalgia and melancholia!"
"In the Jōmon era, you know," continues Uncle,
"tochi-no-mi, the seeds, were carefully stored
by villagers to survive their severe winters."

"In one year, a tochi-no-ki could bear two
to three thousand seeds, which were plump
like Totoro's acorns, certainly carrying more
calories than the same weight of white rice!"

On the way back, Totoro's dropping acorns:
Ichi - ni - san - shi - go -
One seed, two seeds, how many are there?
Roku - shichi - hachi - kyuu -

"No hatred or villains will follow us to death."
"Tell me, Uncle, how do you know?"
"'Acorns of Kiso / for those floating on / my gift,'
writes Borges, that we're merely travellers."

"No, Uncle, no! That's Matsuo Bashō!"
"Listen. Borges writes: 'I've studied every mirror
on this earth, and every mirror reflects me.'"
"No, Uncle. You're wrong! Borges says:
not a mirror's ever reflected him; mirrors—
to Borges, are labyrinths, worldly and ideal."
"You tofu brain!" agitated Uncle, revolting,
"What do you know! Finish your tofu first!"

O tofu, how tenderly you survive in oblivion:
tofu soft cream bubbling on a tofu pudding,
tofu ice-cream melting in the matcha syrup—
these after-hike staples, very calm in foam.

"Ganbatte! Ganbatte!" Somebody in the hill
cheers me up, as if he knows what the end's
like no matter what; then, while moving ahead,
I'm only walking towards the whatsoevers—

I walk, looking around, but nobody's there.
Only is Uncle licking back an adzuki, smiling:
"Our joy wouldn't lie when you eat—"
He bites into his tofu, not elaborating more.

In our mouths there're sediments unmolten,
we've been arguing if they're telling us—
trials are inevitable, or that the fragments
from our sorrows are inevitably unforsaken—

"What tofu-legs you have, you can't walk long!"
groans Uncle. After years, I'm still reminded
of how my legs are as vulnerable as a tofu—
perfectly obedient yet perfectly unreliable.

An adzuki's rolling its head off my tofu.
"What's Uncle's surname before he got adopted?"
"Takanashi!" bellows Mum, "Takanashi!"
"What does it mean?" I ask, very curious.

"Pear tree / little birds play / no hawks—"
"That's it? Is that all?" I mutter.
How're you / adzuki / moshi – moshi?
Where're you heading / moshi – moshi?

Over the hill, shadows move into shadows—
Totoro, will you stay with me tomorrow?
The hawks above us, shrieking—
their wings count: *ichi* - *ni* - *san* -

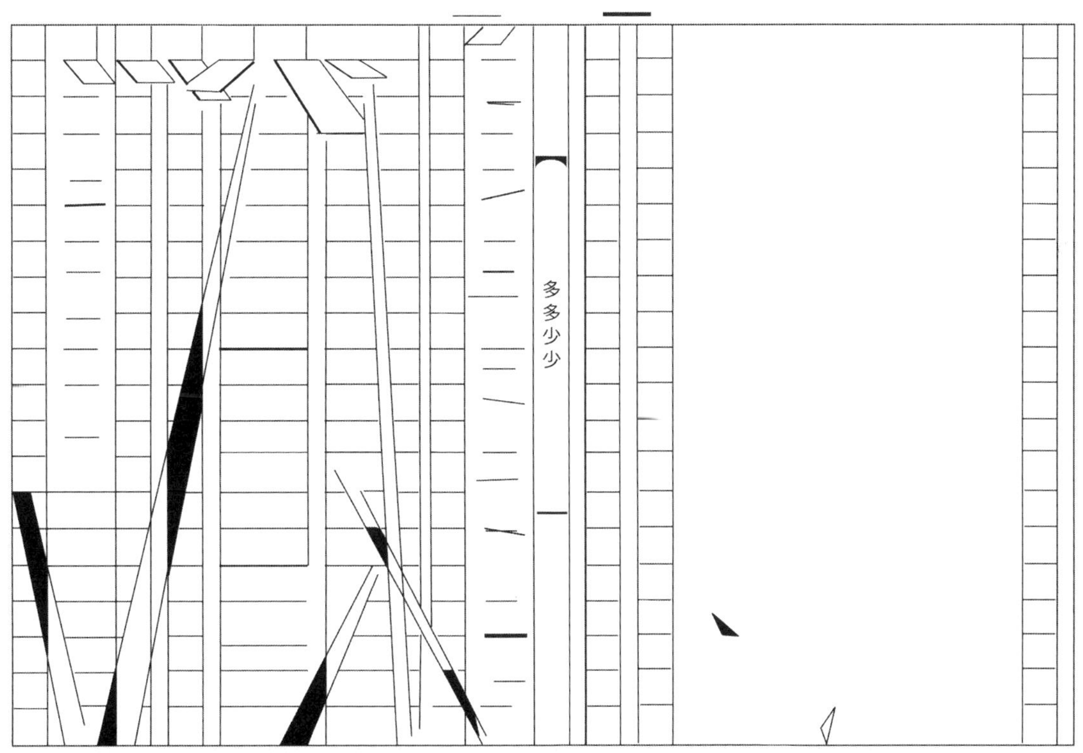

幾多 乘 幾多

ARASHIYAMA, 1994

Towards the sun a shadowed cool

wrestling—

frangipani after frangipani

Curlicues in slow circles—

crickets disappear

grotesque cages of blossoms—

where am I heading to,

when I keep going after you?

TOFU AND THE MONK

In the unquivering quiet,
his knife can't deceive.

He wants to cut out the shape
of a fortune-less life:

karma cancelled—
for a perfect emptiness.

He pockets sadness—
sighs an unreal cloud

for the fated sun to rise.
He defers his smile

until the sun reappears—
like a vaporous lake.

The pot, now, an exit,
each slice turns thinner—

for a second life
in the boiling water.

DUMPLINGS

Cut your carrot into tiny cubes,
crisp and neat as a fistful of luck.

Tear the tomato into cyclic reds,
so its flesh smells like a biome.

Take out the greasy minced pork,
and let your hands be twice oily

as your tomorrows be drenched
in these rich fats of pork belly—

Your brain shouldn't grow grass—
don't think like scallion heads.

Let these white flags boil soft
like your notepad's paper corners.

Knead extra-fatty pork to juice
up the shrimps, like your mother's

grandmother's great grandmother.
Sprinkle a few coriander leaves

or, a few corn kernels. Tell me—
Are you happy? How's your life?

TO RETURN

Choked by coughs I fly
away that vodka flies
like hawks hauling my skull to the vodka that shuns

spires between blunt blades
where the sun dances polka with Svedka,
I'm so stuck that I jump off the hollow—

by humming over the spinning
earth that, how many times, naked,
I, at the centre of this,

like waves of pines and valleys and apologies
hung high over the smoke; and the mirrors
turning me to return to myself, mocking

the sudden breeze as if I were
moon-eyed, across the loose ends
of trees over the dried-out woodland, flying, flying—

BAGPIPES, ST. PATRICK'S DAY

Sparrows preening the sheen,
ruffles and forms in sonorous green.
This afternoon, how shiny, a parade of sequins,
tartans spiral with broken chords.
The trees, drummed up, shuffling
the bellies of air with soft-shell silence
and sombre musings upon the lavish wings—
Grails of white lilies grooming the luminous—
St. Patrick slips in:
Come with me, I'll show
you the world in its broken shadows
open to a new strength.

A PARABLE

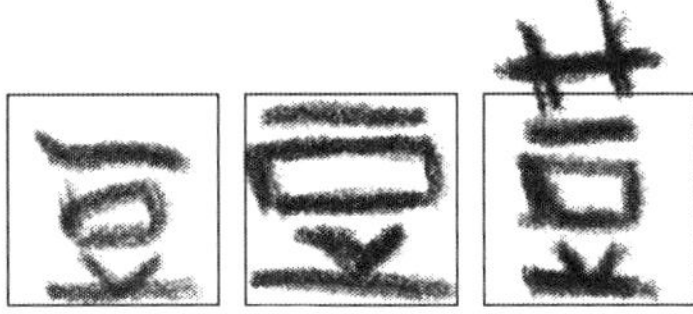

Three hermits mistaken for three
separate words of 豆 secluding
in three solid grids. Three solid

grids mistaken for three prisoners
under three square spotlights
which're for three actors to perform.

HERMIT 1: I am not 豆, but they
insist I am 豆;
and I've to do whatever 豆 does.

HERMIT 2: "What's wrong with you, 豆?"
they ask. "Why don't you do
your homework, go to a university,
be a lawyer or doctor?" again—they ask.

HERMIT 3: I'd grow an antler. Look: 荳.

Mum asks who "they" are.
Miss Wong loves the enchantment.
Uncle Ming doesn't complain.

HERMIT 1:

豆's boiling soft so 豆 sings like rains:

mi - mi - mi - mi - mi - so - so –

Your fate wrapped in tofu turning soft.

HERMIT 2:

豆's brain starts to rain so 豆 sings:

so - so - so - re - mi –

Rains only come when I eat my tofu!

HERMIT 3:

豆 lets 豆 rain so - so - 豆 sings:

mi - mi - mi - mi - mi - so - so –

so - so - so - re - mi – that's 豆's brain!

ALL:

To 豆 and 荳 and 豆 we sing:

Eat your tofu, tofu brain!

Stewed or steamed—

who cares? You're a rare tofu,

like a white, white flower!

mi - mi - mi - mi - mi - so - so –

so - so - so - re - mi –

Of the three hermits,
three mouths in three squares.
Pop a seed into their mouths,
they may grow—
a white, white flower.

Say 豆, your mouth brightly
round, and too, abstrusely round—
Say 豆, protrude, protrude—

You're fed a seed
that you can't
see, like the rain-
studs that are stud-less:

this 豆, a thing-in-itself
sung whole,
like rains grooming holes—

Streets of rabbit-lights,
red, blackout, red-white—
a white, white flower.

to day white w h i t e clutching white what can't stop
you
fu night time

t o f u
what what can can't w h i t e s t o p
I'm t i time stop stop day can't
night night night f o u r
m e corners

of you

of me you

I'm
too

you
t o f u

too
much
tofu Du Fu
eats
tofu

t o f u-
t o day f u-
I'm n i g h t
too

today tonight thoughts shadows
shadows
c a n ' t
stop

night
white
white
w h i t e day
night white
white day
white flower soft
a hand
stop clutching
I
time can't
tofu flower
tofu

OUT OF A BROKEN EGG

Afternoon licks a daub

of egg to the geisha's face,

the yellow shallow—

the connoisseur pretends she's singing summer:

frogs' legs widen lilies, bees burned in the heroic

rise of the theatrical sun, and back

to the wild green. The yellow simmers.

Her lips amused by a simple joke,

the air shunning like a minimalist—

the mosquitoes, nowhere to hide,

fly with a virtue of not destroying a sigh.

It's one of the afternoons far away from lust—

deep in her throat is a long dark corridor.

CUCUMBER AND THE CATBUS CLUB

AFTER JOHN ASHBERY'S "FARM IMPLEMENTS AND RUTABAGAS IN A LANDSCAPE"

A cool breeze over the bento,
the daikon soup, and a few bonito flakes.
"Cucumberish," whistles Shiso, "the window
shines our faces green in Cucumber's fresh flicks—
now, our last days are happily ever-green."
Leavis sighs, his lips glowing thin:

"Cucumber's dying, she's too thin."
"But the gusto," argues Shiso, "over the bento
is sung by Cucumber and the Catbus Club, perfect like her green
pleasure. Let's rock with Cucumber's flakes!"
"Pardon me," Leavis chimes in, "just a few flicks,
my ears flourish like magic drizzles. See, how the window

sees through my veins for me to overhear." Window
gets bewildered, her glass-eyes too thin.
Mr. Shishamo, known as Mr. Willow Leaf Fish, flicks
off the extra oil, says: "All dissonance in this bento—
just starchy blunt ends—and you're merely some cocky veggie flakes
that got me choked on your charred green

nonsense; ah, now, I'm always coughing green!"
In the midday sun, Leavis swipes the window
into halos; he sees under the sea-flakes
of Mr. Willow Leaf Fish a thin-

line riddle: “May the green prosper in the bento!”
Leavis smiles, leaning forth: “Listen, light-flicks

near the end of one’s life are only purposeless flicks
under the sun.” “So—” puzzled Shiso, “in this bruised green
gruel, are we dying?” “Well,” chuckles Leavis, “the bento
conjures up a flimsy, fleeing sense of wakefulness, and the window,
henceforth, keeps us floating; but the *now* we’re in is too thin—
that once we stop talking, we will vanish like flakes.”

Shiso scratches out her flour-flakes,
her headache less heavy after a few flicks
of mossy-ferny sheen. A stranger, wearing a thin
moustache, enquires: “Is today’s cucumber green?”
The sun halfway in, the window’s
starving. “Catbus! Catbus!” a little girl points to her bento—

“This,” grins Shiso, her lips poorly thin, “must be Cucumber’s darling in the bento.”
“This is an omen from cats!” groaning Leavis, “Cucumber’s gonna lose the game of green flicks.”
“Oh goodness,” Mr. Willow Leaf Fish awed, “these windowflakes—”

THE LAST DAYS

You open your mouth, not letting
                    a part of you getting out. You

breathe like a space ripped—
                    the contents within, prior to ruffles,

pouring shadows: the quirks
                    of matter, the rising ruminations,

the dust between flickers. Every
                    breath revisits like a revolt

by inviting more words into chaos. Winds
                    open their mouths, like you speaking:

There, I'll be there, fuller in everything,
                    with no fixed plan upon arriving—

ONE INTIMATE MORNING

The first goldfish breeds lights.

The second one sleeps like a tuft

of lights for being a thoughtful gift.

The third, mindful over the water—

carries itself as a sanctuary.

I comb out the first ray: this morning,

very tenuous in the water;

and the fish trimming every second—

Coiled near their cheeks, the seaweed

reticent in a tussock—

I can't stop admiring its tapering

green; and meanwhile, million mysteries are curling

long at my fingertips.

I'm the enigma at the centre of *now.*

The fish look at me

as if I were their dream. I scatter

more pellets, can't give

more than a little inaudible rain—

NOTES

The manuscript's epigraph comes from Laozi's *Tao Te Ching* translated by Stephen Mitchell.

In "Let's Go Back to Grass Flower Head," "Grass Flower Head" is the literal name of the Chinese botanical radical: 艹

"63 Temple Street, Mong Kok" borrows a line from Laozi's *Tao Te Ching*, translated by Stephen Mitchell. The dialogue with Waiter Kuen is adapted from an episode in the Hong Kong cartoon, *McDull*.

"Dining with Whom?" borrows the pattern of lines from Henri Cole's "Jealousy."

"This Year the Sky" takes the mythic characters of Zhinü and Niulang from the Chinese folktale "The Cowherd and the Weaver Girl."

"A Hinterland within Uncle's Feng Shui Mirror": the Chinese lines quote Eason Chan's song "Shall We Talk."

"Speed Ode" is indebted to Sharon Olds' *Odes*.

"Miss Wong Says" quotes and modifies Wang Wei's poem "Shared Yearning."

In "So, Is That How Light Travels?," the lines of Zhuangzi are taken and modified from his essay "Wandering Where You Will" in *The Book of Chuang Tzu*, translated by Martin Palmer, Elizabeth Breuilly, Chang Wai Ming, and Jay Ramsay.

In "This July Totoro," some of the lines are taken from the works of Jorge Luis Borges, including "Ars Poetica" translated by Harold Morland and "The Aleph" translated by

Norman Thomas di Giovanni and Borges himself. And the line of Matsuo Bashō is translated by David Landis Barnhill.

"To Return" borrows its form from the ending of Susan Stewart's "Wings."

"A Parable": the music "mi - mi - mi - mi - mi - so - so – / so - so - so - re - mi –" and the line "white day white night white flower flower" are taken from a Hong Kong Cantopop—"留白" ("Leave It Blank") sung by Ivana Wong. The phrase "rabbit-light" is taken from Wallace Stevens' "A Rabbit as King of the Ghosts."

"Cucumber and the Catbus Club": Catbus is one of the characters in the Studio Ghibli's animation *My Neighbor Totoro.*

ACKNOWLEDGEMENTS

I am grateful to the editors of the following publications, where these poems, some in earlier and under different titles, originally appeared: *Tupelo Quarterly, Cordite Poetry Review: Online Chapbook Hong Kong Now, Chicago Quarterly Review, Australian Book Review, Voice and Verse Poetry Magazine, Mingled Voices 3: Proverse Poetry Prize Anthology, New Reader Magazine, World Literature Today, Meanjin, Foothill: A Journal of Poetry, Aesthetica Creative Writing Anthology, Atlanta Review*, and *Overland.*

I would also like to thank the judges and committees of the following poetry competitions for their belief in my poems and manuscript during its early stages: "63 Temple Street, Mong Kok," a Co-winner of the Peter Porter Poetry Prize (2019); "This Year the Sky," originally titled "That Space," won a Second Place (ESL Category) in the Oxford Brookes International Poetry Competition (2016); "Cucumber and the Catbus Club," shortlisted for the *Aesthetica* Creative Writing Award (2022); "One Intimate Morning," a Finalist in the *Atlanta Review*'s International Publication Prize (2019); and "Grass Flower Head," which received an Honourable Mention in the Tom Howard/Margaret Reid Poetry Contest (2018). The manuscript, originally titled *Rabbit-Light*, was Highly Commended for the Arts Queensland Thomas Shapcott Poetry Prize (2018). Under a different title, "Grass Flower Head," it was shortlisted for the Puncher & Wattmann Prize for a First Book of Poetry (2018) and selected as a Semi-Finalist for the Brittingham & Felix Pollak Prizes in Poetry (2021).

My deep gratitude goes to the institutions and organizations for their generous support and encouragement. I am most grateful for The University of Queensland's PhD in Creative Writing Programme for giving me such a precious opportunity to pursue my passion in poetry, and for its robust research funding and scholarships, which have made this writing project possible. I am also profoundly thankful to the UQ Library for its initiative in acquiring books that have greatly assisted my writing. My sincere appreciation goes to the Emmanuel College at UQ for offering me a safe and supportive living environment under the Lucy Morris Stevens Scholarship. I am deeply grateful to the New York State Summer Writers Institute for nurturing my writing agility and perseverance. I also want to thank PLAYA for its artist residency, which has inspired me to pursue my writing dream.

I am indebted to the editors of Tupelo Press, Jeffrey Levine, Kristina Marie Darling, and Cassandra Cleghorn, who put faith in my manuscript. Thank you to David Rossitter for your unfailing efforts in bringing the book into shape.

My deepest gratitude to Bronwyn Lea for trusting in my poetry and mentoring me all the way through, and to Ruth Blair for your sincere encouragement and fruitful intellectual discussion. My abiding thanks to my poetry teachers: Page Richards, Judith Beveridge, Martin Harrison, David Brooks, Campbell McGrath, and Henri Cole.

I would also like to thank my mentors, friends, and relatives who have been my bulwarks in my writing journey: Duncan Barlow and Allison Barlow for your spiritual support and laugher; Sarah Sun for your genuine friendship and comfort; Marty Pham for your intelligence and jokes; Timothy Liu for your music and deep conversations; Cynthy Siu for always listening to me; Becky Tsui for your consistently generous advice; my aunt Abby Chu for your love; and my brother Hin for your inspiration.

To my parents: you are the best gifts of my life.

Photo Credit: Sarah Sun

Belle Ling was born and raised in Hong Kong. She was a Co-Winner of the *Australian Book Review*'s Peter Porter Poetry Prize, a fellowship awardee of the PLAYA's Residency, and a Lucy Morris Stevens Scholar awarded by the Emmanuel College at The University of Queensland. Her poetry manuscript, *Rabbit-Light*, was Highly Commended for the Arts Queensland Thomas Shapcott Poetry Prize, and her other poetry collection, *Grass Flower Head*, was shortlisted for the Puncher & Wattmann Prize for a First Book of Poetry. She holds a PhD in Creative Writing from The University of Queensland and a Master of Creative Writing from The University of Sydney. She lives in Hong Kong.